BPP Professional Education
3/34 Co---- Circus
B---- ----- B4 6BN
Phone: 0121 345 9843

GUIDELINES FOR THE ASSESSMENT OF GENERAL DAMAGES IN PERSONAL INJURY CASES

GUIDELINES FOR THE ASSESSMENT OF GENERAL DAMAGES IN PERSONAL INJURY CASES

Fifteenth Edition

Compiled for the

Judicial College

by
THE HON. MRS JUSTICE LAMBERT DBE;
PETER CARSON, SOLICITOR AND DEPUTY DISTRICT JUDGE;
STUART MCKECHNIE QC, BARRISTER;
STEVEN SNOWDEN QC, BARRISTER;
RICHARD WILKINSON, BARRISTER

Foreword by the Rt. Hon. The Lord Burnett of Maldon

OXFORD
UNIVERSITY PRESS

OXFORD
UNIVERSITY PRESS

Great Clarendon Street, Oxford, OX2 6DP,
United Kingdom

Oxford University Press is a department of the University of Oxford.
It furthers the University's objective of excellence in research, scholarship,
and education by publishing worldwide. Oxford is a registered trade mark of
Oxford University Press in the UK and in certain other countries

© Judicial College 2019

The moral rights of the authors have been asserted

Fourteenth Edition published in 2017
Fifteenth Edition published in 2019

Impression: 3

Published in the United States of America by Oxford University Press
198 Madison Avenue, New York, NY 10016, United States of America

British Library Cataloguing in Publication Data
Data available

ISBN 978–0–19–885093–9

Printed and bound in the UK
by CPI Group (UK) Ltd, Croydon, CR0 4YY

Contents

Foreword to the Fifteenth Edition of the Judicial College's Guidelines for the Assessment of General Damages in Personal Injury Cases

There will be few practitioners who can remember the days before the publication of the 1st Edition of these Guidelines in 1992, when those involved in personal injury litigation in the County Courts laboured long and hard to photocopy extracts from *Kemp & Kemp* (it was too heavy to carry) and *Current Law* to deploy in support of an argument over general damages. The aim of the 1st Edition was to consign that practice to history; and it did so. That aim, described by Lord Donaldson of Lymington in his foreword to the 1st Edition, has been achieved.

The Editorial Board do not make the law on general damages but reflect the awards being made by judges in particular by reviewing such reports of assessments of damages as are available. The very success of the Guidelines means that there are fewer such reports.

Nonetheless, awards of general damages for pain, suffering, and loss of amenity do not stand still. They are subject to developing scientific understanding of the causes and consequences of some injuries. Lingering symptoms and pain which in the past were inexplicable may no longer be so. There is scope for judicial development of general damages in some areas and for continuing recalibration to achieve a consistency across the board.

Despite improvements in road safety, the design of vehicles, safety in the workplace, and a more risk averse society, accidents will continue to happen. There will continue to be large volumes of personal injury litigation. As ever, these Guidelines will be the first point of reference for any legal practitioner or litigant seeking to establish the parameters of an award of general damages.

The Right Honourable The Lord Burnett of Maldon
Lord Chief Justice of England and Wales

Foreword to the First Edition
by Lord Donaldson of Lymington

Paradoxical as it may seem, one of the commonest tasks of a judge sitting in a civil court is also one of the most difficult. This is the assessment of general damages for pain, suffering, or loss of the amenities of life. Since no monetary award can compensate in any real sense, these damages cannot be assessed by a process of calculation. Yet whilst no two cases are ever precisely the same, justice requires that there be consistency between awards.

The solution to this dilemma has lain in using the amount of damages awarded in reported cases as guidelines or markers and seeking to slot the particular case into the framework thus provided. This is easier stated than done, because reports of the framework cases are scattered over a variety of publications and not all the awards appear, from the sometimes brief reports, to be consistent with one another. Furthermore some of the older cases are positively misleading unless account is taken of changes in the value of money and the process of revaluation is far from being an exact science.

It was against this background that the Judicial Studies Board set up a working party under the chairmanship of Judge Roger Cox to prepare *Guidelines for the Assessment of General Damages in Personal Injury Cases*. It was not intended to represent, and does not represent, a new or different approach to the problem. Nor is it intended to be a 'ready reckoner' or in any way to fetter the individual judgment which must be brought to bear upon the unique features of each particular case. What it is intended to do, and what it does quite admirably, is to distil the conventional wisdom contained in the reported cases, to supplement it from the collective experience of the working party and to present the result in a convenient, logical and coherent form.

There can be no doubt about the practical value of this report and it has been agreed by the four Heads of Division that it shall be circulated to all judges, recorders and district judges who may be concerned with the assessment of general damages in personal injury cases. We also consider that it should be made available to the two branches of the practising profession and to any others who would be assisted by it.

Judges and practitioners will, as always, remain free to take full account of the amount of damages awarded in earlier cases, but it is hoped that with the publication of this report this will less often be necessary. They will also need to take account of cases reported after the effective date of the working party's report since that report, while to some extent providing a new baseline, is not intended to, and could not, freeze the scale of damages either absolutely or in relative terms as between different categories of loss. May I convey my sincere congratulations to the authors upon the excellent way in which they have performed their task.

Lord Donaldson of Lymington
25 March 1992

Introduction to the Judicial College Guidelines— Fifteenth Edition

I am delighted to have the opportunity to chair the editorial board of this publication. I am one of the few who remember, only too vividly, the days before the Guidelines existed and the many hours spent scouting through Chambers looking for back issues of *Current Law* which might help point me in the right direction on the appropriate level of general damages. I also remember the distinct scepticism which greeted the first edition of the Guidelines published in 1992 and the general sense that such a thin volume could never replace that sift through the reported decisions and provide sufficient and detailed guidance to reflect the huge range of injuries which the courts must compensate in an award of general damages. Within a short time, however, the sceptics were proved wrong. The Guidelines have, now, long been an essential part of the personal injury practitioner's toolkit, providing at the very least the starting point for the evaluation of awards of general damages and often the end point too with any remaining argument being reserved for where, within the bracket, the level of damages should fall.

For the purposes of this edition, the editorial team has undertaken a comprehensive review of the reported decisions over the past two years. In fact, there are remarkably few. In large part this is due to the success of this publication. Its high standing amongst practitioners and the judiciary is the result of all of those who precede me together with the many practitioner experts who have populated the various editorial boards along the way. They have devised injury categories, introducing new sections where advances in medical science have enabled a better understanding of specific injuries, such as chronic pain or injuries resulting in death. They have refined other categories. They have undertaken all the hard work of reviewing relevant reported decisions so that the busy practitioner does not need to. I pay tribute to them all.

The Guidelines remain a distillation of awards of damages that have been and are being, made in the courts. We are all keenly aware that no financial award can compensate in any real sense for physical or mental pain and suffering.

However, one of the objectives of the Guidelines is to achieve consistency in awards for general damages made by the courts, recognizing that it is a book of guidelines and not tramlines and that the assessment of the appropriate level of any award remains the prerogative of the courts.

Since 2017 when the Guidelines were last revised, inflation has continued its slow upward path. The figures in this volume have been adjusted to reflect the general increase in RPI of 7% over the period from May 2017 to June 2019 and have been rounded up or down to provide realistic and practical brackets. As in previous editions, we have considered whether some index other than the RPI should be used to update the figures but again concluded that for present purposes the RPI remains appropriate. However, in the next edition, we will again review whether the rate of increase should appropriately and across the board reflect RPI or some other, and if so what, index. This edition retains figures for general damages with and without the *Simmons v Castle* 10% uplift. There remains only a small number of older cases which will not attract the 10% uplift; however, the collective experience of the editorial team suggests that the number remains sufficient to justify the inclusion of both figures. We are also aware that the use of the Guidelines extends to jurisdictions where the *Simmons* uplift does not apply. For these reasons we have decided to retain both sets of figures, at least for this edition. We are conscious that the readership of the publication is, increasingly, made up of litigants in person. With this in mind we have, where appropriate, tried to simplify some of the injury categories and have provided further explanatory text, in particular in the categories of psychiatric injury. In the next edition we will consider whether it is appropriate and practical to create a separate sub-category of psychiatric injury reflecting awards made to victims of sexual abuse. Our decision will depend in large part upon the reported decisions on such injuries over the life of this edition. It seems to us, however, that there are strong arguments for creating such a sub-category if at all possible, given the particular features which often arise in such cases such as breach of trust, the inability to form or maintain emotional and sexual relationships, the impact on education, and the effect on the victim of the, often, long interval before the fact of the abuse is reported.

As we set out in more detail at the start of Chapters 7 and 13, the Civil Liability Act 2018 received royal assent in December 2018. Part One of that Act includes measures implemented as part of the Government's whiplash reform programme and when coupled with the secondary legislation will provide a tariff for general damages for whiplash injuries which fall within the definition in section 1 of the Act. The Act and associated regulations are intended to come into force in April 2020 subject to the constraints of other parliamentary business. However, the details of the provisions to be implemented remain uncertain and no guarantee can understandably be given as to the precise date of their implementation. At present therefore we can do no more than footnote the existence of the new whiplash damages tariff scheme and note that once enacted the award of general damages for whiplash injuries caught by the Act will be determined by reference to that legislative tariff and not to the Guidelines. We recognize that the legislative scheme in practice may well throw up some interesting issues, not least the approach of the courts to an award for damages for whiplash injuries in combination with other injuries. However, whilst we await reported decisions of damages awards made under the Act, and their relationship with the Guidelines, with interest, it is appropriate to emphasize at this stage that the practical operation of the new damages tariff scheme falls well outside the scope of this publication and will be a matter for judicial determination. It is not for us to dictate or advise upon the practical effect of the scheme.

Finally, I cannot sign off this introduction without some words of thanks. First, to Tim Paviour of the Judicial College who has taken over from Samantha Livsey as co-ordinator of the editorial board and who has, with unstinting good humour and charm, enabled this edition to come to fruition in as short a timescale as possible. Second, my sincere thanks go to my editorial team: Peter Carson, Steven Snowden QC, Stuart McKechnie QC, and Richard Wilkinson whose collective knowledge and expertise is, quite simply, outstanding.

Christina Lambert

Note on 10% Uplift

As explained in previous editions of these Guidelines, one of the consequences of the implementation in 2013 of the *Jackson* reforms to civil litigation was that in most personal injury claims, 'success fees' charged by solicitors to their clients under the terms of a Conditional Fee Agreement ceased to be recoverable from their opponent. Primarily to compensate Claimants for this loss, in *Simmons v Castle* [2012] EWCA Civ 1288; [2013] 1 All ER 334, the Court of Appeal determined that awards of general damages should be uplifted by 10% for all cases in which judgment was given after 1 April 2013, save for those cases where the claimant falls within section 44(6) of the Legal Aid, Sentencing and Punishment of Offenders Act 2012 ('LASPO').

Section 44(6) provides for Claimants who have entered into relevant CFA agreements prior to 1 April 2013 to continue to recover success fees from their opponents. Such Claimants do not benefit from the 10% uplift in general damages.

In the 14th edition we suggested it may no longer be necessary to continue to provide the pre-uplift figures in future editions. Save for mesothelioma claims, where different rules apply, the number of ongoing cases which attract pre-uplift figures is now very modest. However, it is the experience of the editors that some such cases are still working their way through the court system. More significantly, we have received correspondence from lawyers working in other jurisdictions who use the Guidelines but where the '*Simmons*' uplift does not apply.

For these reasons, whilst we recognize that the overwhelming majority of cases will now attract the 10% uplift, we have decided to continue to show both the pre-uplift and '+10% uplift' figures.

Note on Multiple Injuries

The assessment of general damages in multiple injury cases can give rise to special difficulty, in particular in determining the extent to which there is any overlap between injuries and how this should be reflected in the award. An illustration of such difficulties, and guidance as to the approach to be taken, can be found in the Court of Appeal decision in *Sadler v Filipiak* [2011] EWCA Civ 1728. We can do no better than quote in full paragraph 34 of the judgment of Pitchford LJ in that case:

'*It is in my judgment always necessary to stand back from the compilation of individual figures, whether assistance has been derived from comparable cases or from the [Judicial College] guideline advice, to consider whether the award for pain, suffering and loss of amenity should be greater than the sum of the parts in order properly to reflect the combined effect of all the injuries upon the injured person's recovering quality of life or, on the contrary, should be smaller than the sum of the parts in order to remove an element of double counting. In some cases, no doubt a minority, no adjustment will be necessary because the total will properly reflect the overall pain, suffering and loss of amenity endured. In others, and probably the majority, an adjustment and occasionally a significant adjustment may be necessary.*'

1

Injuries Resulting in Death

Fatal accident claims sometimes include an element for pain, suffering, and loss of amenity for the period between injury and death. In some circumstances the awards may be high, for example those relating to asbestos exposure or misdiagnosis of cancer. Others follow extensive periods of disability before death supervenes. In such cases reference should be made to the awards for the underlying injuries or condition, suitably adjusted to reflect the fact (if it be the case) that the claimant knows that death is approaching, and the period of suffering.

Yet there are many cases in which a serious injury is followed relatively quickly by death. Factors that inform the level of general damages include the nature and extent of the injury, the claimant's awareness of his impending death, the extent of pain and suffering, or, in cases where the claimant is unconscious for all or part of the period, loss of amenity. Under s. 1(1)(a) of the Administration of Justice Act 1982 awards may be made for 'mental anguish' (even in the absence of psychiatric injury) caused by fear of curtailment of life: see *Kadir v Mistry* [2014] EWCA Civ 1177.

		with 10% uplift
(A) Full Awareness	£10,700 to £20,320	**£11,770 to £22,350**

Severe burns and lung damage followed by full awareness for a short period and then fluctuating levels of consciousness for between four and five weeks, coupled with intrusive treatment or significant orthopaedic/physical injuries followed by death within a couple of weeks up to 3 months.

		with 10% uplift

(B) Followed by Unconsciousness

£8,970 to £9,100   £9,870 to £10,010

Severe burns and lung damage causing excruciating pain but followed by unconsciousness after 3 hours and death two weeks later.

(C) Immediate Unconsciousness/Death after Six Weeks

£3,210 To £3,750   £3,530 To £4,120

Immediate unconsciousness after injury, and death occurring after six weeks.

(D) Immediate Unconsciousness/Death within One Week

£1,170 to £2,390   £1,290 to £2,620

Immediate unconsciousness, or unconsciousness following very shortly after injury, and death occurring within a week. Where the victim is conscious initially but dies from their injuries the same day an award towards the bottom of the range will be appropriate.

(E) Mental Anguish

£3,980   £4,380

Fear of impending death/reduction in expectation of life.

For the parent of young children suffering such mental anguish for a period of around 3 months.

2

Injuries Involving Paralysis

When assessing awards in cases which fall within this chapter consideration may need to be given to the relevance of scientific/technological developments, balancing as appropriate any restoration of function or reduction in pain that may be achieved against the associated inconvenience or risks.

		with 10% uplift
(a) Tetraplegia (also known as Quadriplegia)	£276,940 to £344,640	**£304,630 to £379,100**

The typical case of tetraplegia attracting an award in the mid-range of this bracket is appropriate for cases in which the injured person is not in physical pain, has full awareness of their disability, has an expectation of life of 25 years or more, has retained powers of speech, sight, and hearing but needs help with bodily functions. At the top end of the bracket will be cases where physical pain is present or where there is a significant effect on senses or ability to communicate. Such cases often involve significant brain damage where degree of insight is a relevant factor: see 3(A)(a). Lack of awareness/ significantly reduced life expectancy will justify a below average award. Other factors bearing on the award include age, the extent of any residual movement, the degree of independence or pain relief (if any) whether through the provision of aids/equipment, treatment, or otherwise, the presence of respiratory issues, and depression.

		with 10% uplift

(b) **Paraplegia**

£186,890 to £242,490 — £205,580 to £266,740

The level of the award within the bracket will be affected by the following considerations:

(i) the presence and extent of pain;

(ii) the degree of independence;

(iii) depression;

(iv) age and life expectancy;

(v) impact on sexual function

The presence of increasing paralysis or the degree of risk that this will occur, for example, from syringomyelia, might take the case above this bracket, as may the presence of other significant injuries. The former might be the subject of a provisional damages order.

(c) **Shorter durations**

£42,090 — £46,300

In cases where death occurs for unrelated reasons within a short period of the accident a lower sum will be awarded. However some 'front-loading' is appropriate. For a young adult claimant suffering paraplegia where death occurs within about 2 years an award of around £42,090 is appropriate (**£46,300** accounting for 10% uplift).

3

Brain and Head Injury

This chapter is primarily concerned with injury that produces physiological dysfunction of the brain as a consequence of injury to the head or brain. The clinical severity of traumatic brain injury is generally (but not exclusively) classified as mild/moderate/severe by reference to the Glasgow Coma Scale and/or the length of loss of consciousness and/or the period of Post-Traumatic Amnesia. The classification will often involve an analysis of any CT/MRI scanning taken in the aftermath of injury. Within this chapter the terms severe, moderate, and mild refer not to the clinical categorization of injury but to the effects of the injury upon the Claimant. The presence and extent of vestibular symptoms may be relevant across the range of brackets. Awards principally reflect the severity of functional outcome. Cases involving birth brain injury resulting in severe cognitive and physical disabilities will often fall in the most serious category.

Although at the interface with Psychiatric injury, diagnosed cases of Post-Concussional Syndrome ('PCS') following injury to the head can also be considered within this chapter. Symptoms commonly include headaches, dizziness, and nausea. Permanent symptoms can result, but most cases resolve within two years. Awards should reflect the nature and severity of symptoms rather than any diagnostic label.

(A) Brain Damage

		with 10% uplift
(a) Very Severe Brain Damage	£240,590 to £344,640	**£264,650 to £379,100**

In cases at the top of this bracket there may be some ability to follow basic commands, recovery of eye opening and return of sleep and waking patterns and postural reflex movement. There will be little, if any, evidence of meaningful response to environment, little or no language function, double incontinence, and the need for full-time nursing care.

5

The level of the award within the bracket will be affected by:

  (i) the degree of insight, if any;

  (ii) life expectancy;

  (iii) the extent of physical limitations;

  (iv) requirement for gastrostomy for feeding;

  (v) sensory impairment;

  (vi) ability to communicate with or without assistive technology;

  (vii) extent of any behavioural problems;

  (viii) the presence of epilepsy and how well it is controlled.

This bracket is likely to include cases involving quadriplegic cerebral palsy causing severe cognitive and physical disabilities. The top of the bracket will be appropriate only where there is significant effect on the senses and severe physical limitation.

This bracket will also include cases involving 'locked in' syndrome with substantially restricted life expectancy. Cases resulting in a permanent vegetative or minimally conscious state with life expectancy in excess of 15 years are likely to fall towards the lower end of this bracket.

		with 10% uplift
(b) Moderately Severe Brain Damage	£186,890 to £240,590	**£205,580 to £264,650**

The injured person will be very seriously disabled. There will be substantial dependence

6

on others and a need for constant professional and other care. Disabilities may be
physical, for example, limb paralysis, or cognitive, with marked impairment of intellect
and personality. Cases otherwise within (a)
above may fall into this bracket if life expectancy has been greatly reduced. Where
there is a risk of associated future development of other severe medical problems
such as blindness an award in excess of
the bracket would be justified.

The level of the award within the bracket will
be affected by the following considerations:

(i)   the degree of insight, if any;

(ii) life expectancy;

(iii) the extent of physical limitations and
      potential for future deterioration;

(iv) the degree of dependence on others;

(v)   ability to communicate;

(vi) extent of any behavioural problems;

(vii) epilepsy or a significant risk of epilepsy
      (unless a provisional damages order
      provides for this risk).

Cases resulting in a permanent vegetative or
minimally conscious state with severely reduced life expectancy are likely to fall within
this bracket. Where there is a persistent vegetative state and death occurs very soon after
the injuries were suffered the award will be
solely for loss of amenity and will fall below
this bracket.

(c) Moderate Brain Damage

This category is distinguished from (b) by the fact that the degree of dependence is markedly lower.

		with 10% uplift
(i) Cases in which there is moderate to severe intellectual deficit, a personality change, an effect on sight, speech, and senses with a significant risk of epilepsy, and no prospect of employment.	£128,060 to £186,890	£140,870 to £205,580
(ii) Cases in which there is a moderate to modest intellectual deficit, the ability to work is greatly reduced if not removed, and there is some risk of epilepsy (unless a provisional damages order provides for this risk).	£77,410 to £128,060	£85,150 to £140,870
(iii) Cases in which concentration and memory are affected, the ability to work is reduced, where there is a small risk of epilepsy, and any dependence on others is very limited.	£36,740 to £77,410	£40,410 to £85,150

(d) Less Severe Brain Damage

£13,070 to £36,740   £14,380 to £40,410

In these cases the injured person will have made a good recovery and will be able to take part in normal social life and to return to work. There may not have been a restoration of all normal functions so there may still be persisting problems such as poor concentration and memory or disinhibition of mood, which may interfere with lifestyle, leisure activities, and future work prospects. At the top of this bracket there may be a small risk of epilepsy.

The level of the award within the bracket will be affected by:

(i) the extent and severity of the initial injury;

(ii) the extent of any continuing, and possibly permanent, disability;

(iii) the extent of any personality change;

(iv) depression.

	with 10% uplift

(e) Minor Brain or Head Injury

£1,880 to £10,890 — **£2,070 to £11,980**

In these cases brain damage, if any, will have been minimal.

The level of the award will be affected by the following considerations:

(i) the severity of the initial injury;

(ii) the period taken to recover from any symptoms;

(iii) the extent of continuing symptoms;

(iv) the presence or absence of headaches.

The bottom of the bracket will reflect full recovery within a few weeks.

(B) Epilepsy

(a) Established Grand Mal

£87,010 to £128,060 — **£95,710 to £140,870**

		with 10% uplift

(b) **Established Petit Mal**

£46,780 to £112,130 — **£51,460 to £123,340**

The level of the award within these brackets will be affected by the following factors:

(i) whether attacks are successfully controlled by medication and the extent to which the need for medication is likely to persist;

(ii) the extent to which the appreciation of life is blunted by such medication;

(iii) the effect on working and/or social life;

(iv) the existence of associated behavioural problems;

(v) the prognosis.

(c) **Other Epileptic Conditions**

£9,080 to £22,440 — **£9,990 to £24,680**

Cases where there are one or two discrete epileptic episodes, or a temporary resurgence of epilepsy, but there is no risk of further recurrence beyond that applicable to the population at large. The level of the award within the bracket will be affected by the extent of any consequences of the attacks on, for example, education, sporting activities, working and social life, and their duration.

4

Psychiatric and Psychological Damage

This chapter covers those cases where there is a recognizable psychiatric injury. In part (A) of this chapter some of the brackets contain an element of compensation for post-traumatic stress disorder. This is of course not a universal feature of cases of psychiatric injury and hence a number of the awards upon which the brackets are based did not reflect it. Where it does figure any award will tend towards the upper end of the bracket. Cases where post-traumatic stress disorder is the sole psychiatric condition are dealt with in part (B) of this chapter. Where cases arise out of sexual and/or physical abuse in breach of parental, family, or other trust, involving victims who are young and/or vulnerable, awards will tend to be at the upper end of the relevant bracket to take into account (A) (vii) below.

(A) Psychiatric Damage Generally

The factors to be taken into account in valuing claims of this nature are as follows:

(i) the injured person's ability to cope with life, education, and work;

(ii) the effect on the injured person's relationships with family, friends, and those with whom he or she comes into contact;

(iii) the extent to which treatment would be successful;

(iv) future vulnerability;

(v) prognosis;

(vi) whether medical help has been sought;

(vii) Claims relating to sexual and physical abuse usually include a significant aspect of psychiatric or psychological damage. The brackets discussed in this chapter provide a useful starting point in the assessment of general damages in such cases. It should not be forgotten, however, that this aspect of the injury is likely to form only part of the injury for which damages will be awarded. Many cases include physical or sexual abuse and injury. Others have an element of false imprisonment. The fact of an abuse of trust is relevant to the award of damages. A further feature, which distinguishes these cases from most involving psychiatric damage, is that there may have been a long period during which the effects of the abuse were undiagnosed, untreated, unrecognized, or even denied. Awards should take into account not only the psychiatric effects of the abuse on the injured party but also the immediate effects of the abuse at the time that it was perpetrated, including feelings of degradation. Aggravated damages may be appropriate. Cases of prolonged and frequent physical and sexual abuse of a child over many years by a person in a position of trust, involving penetrative violation, are likely to fall into (A)(a) or (B)(a) and reflect aggravated damages, leading to an award towards the top end of the bracket.

		with 10% uplift

(a) **Severe**

$£46,780$ to $£98,750$ — **£51,460 to £108,620**

In these cases the injured person will have marked problems with respect to factors (i) to (iv) above and the prognosis will be very poor.

(b) **Moderately Severe**

$£16,270$ to $£46,780$ — **£17,900 to £51,460**

In these cases there will be significant problems associated with factors (i) to (iv) above but the prognosis will be much more optimistic than in (a) above. While there are awards which support both extremes of this bracket, the majority are somewhere near the middle of the bracket. Cases involving psychiatric injury following a negligent stillbirth or the traumatic birth of a child will often fall within this bracket. Cases of work-related stress resulting in a permanent or long-standing disability preventing a return to comparable employment would appear to come within this category.

(c) **Moderate**

$£5,000$ to $£16,270$ — **£5,500 to £17,900**

While there may have been the sort of problems associated with factors (i) to (iv) above there will have been marked improvement by trial and the prognosis will be good.

Cases of work-related stress may fall within this category if symptoms are not prolonged.

		with 10% uplift

(d) Less Severe — £1,310 to £5,000 / **£1,440 to £5,500**

The level of the award will take into consideration the length of the period of disability and the extent to which daily activities and sleep were affected. Cases falling short of a specific phobia or disorder such as travel anxiety when associated with minor physical symptoms may be found in the Minor Injuries chapter.

(B) Post-Traumatic Stress Disorder

Cases within this category are exclusively those where there is a specific diagnosis of a reactive psychiatric disorder following an event which creates psychological trauma in response to actual or threatened death, serious injury, or sexual violation. The guidelines below have been compiled by reference to cases which variously reflect the criteria established in the 4th and then 5th editions of *Diagnostic and Statistical Manual of Mental Disorders* (DSM-IV-TR and DSM-5). The symptoms may include nightmares, flashbacks, sleep disturbance, avoidance, mood disorders, suicidal ideation, and hyper-arousal. Symptoms of hyper-arousal can affect basic functions such as breathing, pulse rate, and bowel and/or bladder control.

(a) Severe — £51,070 to £85,880 / **£56,180 to £94,470**

Such cases will involve permanent effects which prevent the injured person from working at all or at least from functioning at anything approaching the pre-trauma level. All aspects of the life of the injured person will be badly affected.

14

		with 10% uplift
(b) Moderately Severe	£19,750 to £51,070	**£21,730 to £56,180**

This category is distinct from (a) above because of the better prognosis which will be for some recovery with professional help. However, the effects are still likely to cause significant disability for the foreseeable future. While there are awards which support both extremes of this bracket, the majority are between £24,540 and £31,660 (**£26,990 and £34,830** accounting for 10% uplift).

(c) Moderate	£6,980 to £19,750	**£7,680 to £21,730**

In these cases the injured person will have largely recovered and any continuing effects will not be grossly disabling.

(d) Less Severe	£3,370 to £6,980	**£3,710 to £7,680**

In these cases a virtually full recovery will have been made within one to two years and only minor symptoms will persist over any longer period.

5

Injuries Affecting the Senses

(A) Injuries Affecting Sight

Damages for loss of sight in one eye are likely to be awarded on a provisional basis to allow for the risk of deterioration or loss of sight in the remaining eye.

			with 10% uplift
(a)	Total Blindness and Deafness	In the region of £344,640	**In the region of £379,100**
	Such cases must be considered as ranking with the most devastating injuries.		
(b)	Total Blindness	In the region of £229,260	**In the region of £252,180**
(c)	Loss of Sight in One Eye with Reduced Vision in the Remaining Eye		
	(i) Where there is serious risk of further deterioration in the remaining eye, going beyond some risk of sympathetic ophthalmia.	£81,910 to £153,390	**£90,100 to £168,730**
	(ii) Where there is reduced vision in the remaining eye and/or additional problems such as double vision.	£54,550 to £90,400	**£60,010 to £99,440**

		with 10% uplift

(d) Total Loss of One Eye

£46,780 to £56,080   £51,460 to £61,690

The level of the award within the bracket will depend on age, psychiatric consequences, and cosmetic effect.

(e) Complete Loss of Sight in One Eye

£42,030 to £46,780   £46,240 to £51,460

This award takes account of some risk of sympathetic ophthalmia. The upper end of the bracket is appropriate where there is scarring in the region of the eye which is not sufficiently serious to merit a separate award.

(f) Cases of serious but incomplete loss of vision in one eye without significant risk of loss or reduction of vision in the remaining eye, or where there is constant double vision. A case of constant blurred vision and sensitivity to light in both eyes requiring constant wearing of dark glasses would be at the top of the bracket.

£20,210 to £33,600   £22,230 to £36,960

(g) Minor but permanent impairment of vision in one or both eyes, including cases where there is some double vision, which may not be constant, and cases of permanent sensitivity to bright light but not sufficient to require constant wearing of dark glasses.

£7,780 to £17,900   £8,550 to £19,690

17

		with 10% uplift

(h) Minor Eye Injuries

£3,370 to £7,460 — **£3,710 to £8,200**

In this bracket fall cases of minor injuries, such as being struck in the eye, exposure to fumes including smoke, or being splashed by liquids, causing initial pain and some temporary interference with vision.

(i) Transient Eye Injuries

£1,880 to £3,370 — **£2,070 to £3,710**

In these cases the injured person will have recovered completely within a few weeks.

(B) Deafness/Tinnitus

The word 'deafness' is used to embrace total and partial hearing loss. In assessing awards for hearing loss regard must be had to the following:

(i) whether the injury is one that has an immediate effect, allowing no opportunity to adapt, or whether it occurred over a period of time, as in noise exposure cases;

(ii) whether the injury or disability is one which the injured person suffered at an early age so that it has had or will have an effect on his or her speech (and will be suffered for a longer period), or is one that is suffered in later life;

(iii) whether the injury or disability affects balance;

(iv) the impact of the hearing loss on occupation;

(v) in cases of noise-induced hearing loss (NIHL) age is of particular relevance as noted in paragraph (d) below;

(vi) tinnitus may be suffered alone, rather than associated with NIHL.

Note also that the cases which form the basis of these brackets were decided before recent advances in medical science, such as cochlear implants which can in some cases restore total deafness to almost full hearing when worn.

		with 10% uplift
(a) Total Deafness and Loss of Speech	£93,540 to £120,040	£102,890 to £132,040

Such cases arise, for example, where deafness has occurred at an early age (for example, rubella infection) so as to prevent or seriously to affect the development of normal speech.

(b) Total Deafness	£77,430 to £93,540	£85,170 to £102,890

The lower end of the bracket is appropriate for cases where there is no speech deficit or tinnitus. The higher end is appropriate for cases involving both of these.

(c) Total Loss of Hearing in One Ear	£26,710 to £38,850	£29,380 to £42,730

Cases will tend towards the higher end of the bracket where there are associated problems, such as tinnitus, dizziness, or headaches.

(d) Partial Hearing Loss and/or Tinnitus

This category covers the bulk of deafness cases which usually result from exposure to noise at work over a prolonged period. The disability is not to be judged simply by the total measurement of hearing loss; there is often a degree of tinnitus present and age is particularly relevant because impairment of hearing affects most people in the fullness of time and impacts both upon causation and upon valuation, such that the amount of noise-induced hearing loss ('NIHL') is likely to be less than an individual's total hearing loss.

			with 10% uplift
(i)	Severe tinnitus and NIHL	£25,350 to £38,850	£27,890 to £42,730
(ii)	Moderate tinnitus and NIHL or moderate to severe tinnitus or NIHL alone	£12,700 to £25,350	£13,970 to £27,890
(iii)	Mild tinnitus with some NIHL	£10,750 to £12,700	£11,820 to £13,970
(iv)	Mild tinnitus alone or mild NIHL alone	Around £10,000	Around £11,000
(v)	Slight or occasional tinnitus with slight NIHL	£6,280 to £10,750	£6,910 to £11,820
(vi)	Slight NIHL without tinnitus or slight tinnitus without NIHL	Up to £5,980	Up to £6,580

(C) Impairment of Taste and Smell

It is rare to find an injury which causes loss of taste and/or smell alone. Such symptoms are usually associated with brain injury or infection, in which case regard should be had to the guidelines for those injuries.

		with 10% uplift
(a) Total Loss of Taste and Smell	In the region of £33,430	In the region of £36,770
(b) Total Loss of Smell and Significant Loss of Taste	£28,070 to £33,430	£30,870 to £36,770

(b) **Total Loss of Smell and Significant Loss of Taste**

It must be remembered that in nearly all cases of loss of smell there is some impairment of taste. Such cases fall into the next bracket.

(c) Loss of Smell	£21,320 to £28,070	£23,460 to £30,870
(d) Loss of Taste	£16,380 to £21,320	£18,020 to £23,460

6

Injuries to Internal Organs

(A) Chest Injuries

This is a specially difficult area because the majority of awards relate to industrial *disease* (see (B) below) as distinct from traumatic *injury*. Cases of traumatic damage to, or loss of, a lung are comparatively rare, and the range is very wide.

The levels of awards within the brackets set out below will be affected by:

  (i) age and gender;

 (ii) scarring;

(iii) the effect on the capacity to work and enjoy life;

(iv) the effect on life expectancy.

			with 10% uplift
(a)	The worst type of case will be of total removal of one lung and/or serious heart damage with serious and prolonged pain and suffering and permanent significant scarring.	£85,880 to £128,060	£94,470 to £140,870
(b)	Traumatic injury to chest, lung(s), and/or heart causing permanent damage, impairment of function, physical disability, and reduction of life expectancy.	£56,100 to £85,880	£61,710 to £94,470

			with 10% uplift
(c)	Damage to chest and lung(s) causing some continuing disability.	£26,710 to £46,780	£29,380 to £51,460
(d)	A relatively simple injury (such as a single penetrating wound) causing some permanent damage to tissue but with no significant long-term effect on lung function.	£10,750 to £15,320	£11,820 to £16,860
(e)	Toxic fume/smoke inhalation, leaving some residual damage, not serious enough to interfere permanently with lung function.	£4,540 to £10,750	£5,000 to £11,820
(f)	Injuries leading to collapsed lungs from which a full and uncomplicated recovery is made.	£1,880 to £4,540	£2,060 to £5,000
(g)	Fractures of ribs or soft tissue injuries causing serious pain and disability over a period of weeks only.	Up to £3,370	Up to £3,710

(B) Lung Disease

The level of the appropriate award for lung disease necessarily, and often principally, reflects the prognosis for what is frequently a worsening condition and/or the risk of the development of secondary sequelae.

Most of the reported cases are of asbestos-related disease (as to which see (C) below) but, save for asthma (which is also dealt with separately in (D) below), the brackets set out are intended to encompass all other lung disease cases irrespective of causation, for example silicosis and pneumoconiosis. In many cases falling under this head provisional awards will be appropriate. At the upper end of the range where serious disabling consequences will already be present, and the prognosis is likely to be relatively clear such an award may not be appropriate. Furthermore, in some cases awards may be enhanced where classifiable psychiatric illness is present.

			with 10% uplift
(a)	For a young person with serious disability where there is a probability of progressive worsening leading to premature death.	£85,880 to £115,940	£94,470 to £127,530
(b)	Lung cancer (typically in an older person) causing severe pain and impairment both of function and of quality of life. Practitioners may find some of the factors set out in (C)(a) useful in determining variations within the bracket.	£59,730 to £83,050	£65,710 to £91,350
(c)	Disease, e.g., emphysema, causing significant and worsening lung function and impairment of breathing, prolonged and frequent coughing, sleep disturbance, and restriction of physical activity and employment.	£46,740 to £59,730	£51,420 to £65,710
(d)	Breathing difficulties (short of disabling breathlessness) requiring fairly frequent use of an inhaler; where there is inability to tolerate a smoky environment and an uncertain prognosis but already significant effect on social and working life.	£26,710 to £46,780	£29,380 to £51,460

			with 10% uplift
(e)	Bronchitis and wheezing not causing serious symptoms; little or no serious or permanent effect on working or social life; varying levels of anxiety about the future.	£17,740 to £26,710	£19,510 to £29,380
(f)	Some slight breathlessness with no effect on working life and the likelihood of substantial and permanent recovery within a few years of the exposure to the cause or the aggravation of an existing condition.	£9,080 to £17,740	£9,990 to £19,510
(g)	Provisional awards for cases otherwise falling within (e) and (f) where the provisional award excludes any risk of malignancy, the extent of anxiety being a factor.	£4,540 to £15,430	£5,000 to £16,980
(h)	Temporary aggravation of bronchitis or other chest problems resolving within a very few months.	£1,880 to £4,540	£2,070 to £5,000

(C) Asbestos-Related Disease

Mesothelioma, lung cancer, and asbestosis are the most serious of these. Mesothelioma is typically of shorter duration than either of the other two and often proves fatal within a matter of months from first diagnosis. Lung cancer and asbestosis are likely to have a fatal outcome, but the symptoms often endure for several years. Most of the recent reported cases concern mesothelioma. Cases of lung cancer and asbestosis may result in similar levels of symptoms to mesothelioma, which may justify awards in excess of the suggested upper brackets for those conditions.

		with 10% uplift
(a) Mesothelioma causing severe pain and impairment of both function and quality of life. This may be of the pleura (the lung lining) or of the peritoneum (the lining of the abdominal cavity); the latter being typically more painful. There are a large number of factors which will affect the level of award within the bracket. These include but are not limited to duration of pain and suffering; extent and effects of invasive investigations; extent and effects of radical surgery, chemotherapy, and radiotherapy; whether the mesothelioma is peritoneal or pleural; the extent to which the tumour has spread to encase the lungs and where other organs become involved causing additional pain and/or breathlessness; the level of the symptoms; domestic circumstances; age, level of activity, and previous state of health; extent of life loss; and concern for spouse and/or children following death. Most reported decisions other than those involving extremely short periods of symptoms or very elderly claimants fall within the middle and upper parts of the bracket. *Note that where mesothelioma cases are still dealt with under pre-LASPO conditional fee agreements, the column without the 10% uplift is applicable.*	£59,730 to £107,410	£65,710 to £118,150

		with 10% uplift
(b) Lung cancer, again a disease proving fatal in most cases, the symptoms of which may not be as painful as those of mesothelioma, but more protracted. As with (B)(b) above, practitioners may find some of the factors in C(a) above useful in determining variations within the bracket.	£59,730 to £83,050	£65,710 to £91,350
(c) Asbestosis and pleural thickening—where the level of disability attributable to asbestos will be in excess of 10% causing progressive symptoms of breathlessness by reducing lung function. Awards at the lower end of the bracket will be applicable where the condition is relatively static. Higher awards will be applicable where the condition has progressed or is likely to progress to cause more severe breathlessness. Awards at the top end of the bracket will be applicable where mobility and quality of life has or is likely to become significantly impaired and/or life expectancy significantly reduced. This is a wide bracket and the extent of respiratory disability will be highly significant with disabilities of 10–30% being at the lower end, 30–50% in the middle, and in excess of 50% at the higher end.	£32,780 to £90,300	£36,060 to £99,330
(d) Asbestosis and pleural thickening—where the level of respiratory disability/lung function impairment attributable to asbestos is 1–10%.	£12,860 to £32,780	£14,140 to £36,060

The level of award will be influenced by whether it is to be final or on a provisional basis and also the extent of anxiety.

(D) Asthma

	with 10% uplift

(a) Severe and permanent disabling asthma, causing prolonged and regular coughing, disturbance of sleep, severe impairment of physical activity and enjoyment of life, and where employment prospects, if any, are grossly restricted.

£36,740 to £56,100 — £40,410 to £61,710

(b) Chronic asthma causing breathing difficulties, the need to use an inhaler from time to time, and restriction of employment prospects, with uncertain prognosis.

£22,440 to £36,700 — £24,680 to £40,370

(c) Bronchitis and wheezing, affecting working or social life, with the likelihood of substantial recovery within a few years of the exposure to the cause.

£16,380 to £22,440 — £18,020 to £24,680

(d) Relatively mild asthma-like symptoms often resulting, for instance, from exposure to harmful irritating vapour.

£9,080 to £16,380 — £9,990 to £18,020

(e) Mild asthma, bronchitis, colds, and chest problems (usually resulting from unfit housing or similar exposure, particularly in cases of young children) treated by a general practitioner and resolving within a few months.

Up to £4,390 — Up to £4,830

(E) Reproductive System: Male

(a) (i) Total Loss of Reproductive Organs

In excess of £131,290 — In excess of £144,420

		with 10% uplift

(ii) Cases of orchidectomy with some psychological consequences but without loss of sexual function or impotence. — £17,120 to £19,260 — **£18,830 to £21,190**

(b) Impotence

(i) Total impotence and loss of sexual function and sterility in the case of a young man. — In the region of £126,550 — **In the region of £139,210**

The level of the award will depend on:

(1) age;

(2) psychological reaction and the effect on social and domestic life.

(ii) Impotence which is likely to be permanent, in the case of a middle-aged man with children. — £36,700 to £66,890 — **£40,370 to £73,580**

(c) Cases of sterility usually fall into one of two categories: surgical, chemical, and disease cases (which involve no traumatic injury or scarring) and traumatic injuries (frequently caused by assaults) which are often aggravated by scarring.

(i) The most serious cases merit awards up to — £120,040 — **£132,040**

(ii) The bottom of the range is the case of the much older man and merits an award of about — £16,000 — **£17,600**

			with 10% uplift

(d) An uncomplicated case of sterility without impotence and without any aggravating features for a young man without children. — £47,830 to £60,880 — **£52,620 to £66,970**

(e) A similar case but involving a family man who might have intended to have more children. — £20,210 to £26,710 — **£22,230 to £29,380**

(f) Cases where the sterility amounts to little more than an 'insult'. — In the region of £5,630 — **In the region of £6,190**

(F) Reproductive System: Female

The level of awards in this area will typically depend on:

(i) whether or not the affected woman already has children and/or whether the intended family was complete;

(ii) scarring;

(iii) depression or psychological scarring;

(iv) whether a foetus was aborted.

(a) Infertility whether by reason of injury or disease, with severe depression and anxiety, pain, and scarring. — £98,010 to £144,520 — **£107,810 to £158,970**

(b) Infertility resulting from failure to diagnose ectopic pregnancy not included in section (a) above but where there are resulting medical complications. The upper end of the bracket will be appropriate where those medical complications are significant. — £29,050 to £87,140 — **£31,950 to £95,850**

			with 10% uplift

(c) Infertility without any medical complication and where the injured person already has children. The upper end of the bracket is appropriate in cases where there is significant psychological damage.

£15,320 to £31,350 — **£16,860 to £34,480**

(d) Infertility where the injured person would not have had children in any event (for example, because of age).

£5,630 to £10,750 — **£6,190 to £11,820**

(e) Failed sterilization leading to unwanted pregnancy where there is no serious psychological impact or depression.

In the region of £8,700 — **In the region of £9,570**

(f) Where delay in diagnosing ectopic pregnancy but fertility not affected. Award dependant on extent of pain, suffering, bleeding, whether blood transfusion required, anxiety and adjustment disorder, and whether there is resultant removal of one of the fallopian tubes.

£2,890 to £17,430 — **£3,180 to £19,170**

(G) Digestive System

The risk of associated damage to the reproductive organs is frequently encountered in cases of this nature and requires separate consideration.

(a) Damage Resulting from Traumatic Injury

(i) Severe damage with continuing pain and discomfort.

£36,700 to £52,810 — **£40,370 to £58,100**

		with 10% uplift
(ii) Serious non-penetrating injury causing long-standing or permanent complications, for example, severe indigestion, aggravated by physical strain.	£14,320 to £23,680	£15,750 to £26,050
(iii) Penetrating stab wounds or industrial laceration or serious seat-belt pressure cases.	£5,630 to £10,750	£6,190 to £11,820

(b) Illness/Damage Resulting from Non-traumatic Injury, e.g. Food Poisoning

There will be a marked distinction between those, comparatively rare, cases having a long-standing or even permanent effect on quality of life and those in which the only continuing symptoms may be allergy to specific foods and the attendant risk of short-term illness.

(i) Severe toxicosis causing serious acute pain, vomiting, diarrhoea, and fever, requiring hospital admission for some days or weeks and some continuing incontinence, haemorrhoids, and irritable bowel syndrome, having a significant impact on ability to work and enjoyment of life.	£32,780 to £44,790	£36,060 to £49,270
(ii) Serious but short-lived food poisoning, diarrhoea, and vomiting diminishing over two to four weeks with some remaining discomfort and disturbance of bowel function and impact on sex life and enjoyment of food over a few years. Any such symptoms having these consequences and lasting for longer, even indefinitely, are likely to merit an award between the top of this bracket and the bottom of the bracket in (i) above.	£8,140 to £16,380	£8,950 to £18,020

		with 10% uplift

(iii) Food poisoning causing significant discomfort, stomach cramps, alteration of bowel function and fatigue. Hospital admission for some days with symptoms lasting for a few weeks but complete recovery within a year or two. — £3,370 to £8,140 — £3,710 to £8,950

(iv) Varying degrees of disabling pain, cramps, and diarrhoea continuing for some days or weeks. — £780 to £3,370 — £860 to £3,710

(H) Kidney

(a) Serious and permanent damage to or loss of both kidneys. — £144,520 to £179,530 — £158,970 to £197,480

(b) Where there is a significant risk of future urinary tract infection or other total loss of natural kidney function. — Up to £54,600 — Up to £60,050

Such cases will invariably carry with them substantial future medical expenses, which in this field are particularly high.

(c) Loss of one kidney with no damage to the other. — £26,260 to £38,280 — £28,880 to £42,110

(I) Bowels

(a) In cases involving double incontinence namely total loss of natural bowel function and complete loss of urinary function and control, together with other medical complications. — Up to £157,150 — Up to £172,860

			with 10% uplift
(b)	Total loss of natural function and dependence on colostomy, depending on age.	Up to £128,060	Up to **£140,870**
(c)	Faecal urgency and passive incontinence persisting after surgery and causing embarrassment and distress, typically following injury giving birth	In the region of £68,180	**In the region of £75,000**
(d)	Severe abdominal injury causing impairment of function and often necessitating temporary colostomy (leaving disfiguring scars) and/or restriction on employment and on diet.	£38,040 to £59,490	**£41,850 to £65,440**
(e)	Penetrating injuries causing some permanent damage but with an eventual return to natural function and control.	£10,750 to £20,880	**£11,820 to £22,970**

(J) Bladder

It is perhaps surprising that awards in cases of loss of bladder function have often been higher than awards for injury to the bowels. This is probably because bladder injuries frequently result from carcinogenic exposure.

(a)	In cases involving double incontinence namely total loss of natural bowel function and complete loss of urinary function and control, together with other medical complications.	Up to £157,150	Up to **£172,860**
(b)	Complete loss of function and control.	Up to £120,040	Up to **£132,040**

34

			with 10% uplift

(c) Serious impairment of control with some pain and incontinence.

£54,600 to £68,190   **£60,050 to £75,010**

(d) Where there has been almost a complete recovery but some fairly long-term interference with natural function.

£19,980 to £26,710   **£21,970 to £29,380**

The cancer risk cases still occupy a special category and can properly attract awards at the top of the ranges even where natural function continues for the time being. If the prognosis is firm and reliable the award will reflect any loss of life expectancy, the level of continuing pain and suffering, and most significantly the extent to which the injured person has to live with the knowledge of the consequences which his or her death will have for others. The appropriate award for the middle-aged family man or woman whose life expectancy is reduced by 15 or 20 years is £44,110 to £64,990 (**£48,520** to **£71,490** accounting for 10% uplift).

(K) Spleen

(a) Loss of spleen where there is continuing risk of internal infection and disorders due to the damage to the immune system.

£17,740 to £22,440   **£19,510 to £24,680**

(b) Where the above risks are not present or are minimal.

£3,710 to £7,380   **£4,080 to £8,110**

(L) Hernia

			with 10% uplift
(a)	Continuing pain and/or limitation on physical activities, sport, or employment, after repair.	£12,700 to £20,620	£13,970 to £22,680
(b)	Direct (where there was no pre-existing weakness) inguinal hernia, with some risk of recurrence, after repair.	£5,980 to £7,780	£6,580 to £8,550
(c)	Uncomplicated indirect inguinal hernia, possibly repaired, and with no other associated abdominal injury or damage.	£2,900 to £6,170	£3,180 to £6,790

7

Orthopaedic Injuries

The Civil Liability Act 2018 ('the Act') received royal assent in December 2018. Part 1 of the Act provides for the introduction of a fixed tariff scheme for general damages awards for whiplash injuries (and including minor psychological injuries) lasting for up to two years as a consequence of a road traffic accident. At the time of publication of the 15th edition of these Guidelines, the provisions of Part 1 of the Act are not yet in force. The current intended implementation date is April 2020. Whenever in fact implemented, it is understood the new tariff regime will apply only to accidents occurring after that date. The guidelines set out below will then cease to apply to those cases caught by the Act. A definition of injuries will be contained in the Act and any accompanying Regulations. The tariff will not apply to claims brought by motorcyclists or their passengers, cyclists, pedestrians, or other road users who are not using a mechanically propelled motor vehicle. Readers will need to refer to the legislation and Regulations to determine whether and to what extent individual cases come within the scope of the new legislation and for details of the applicable tariff.

(A) Neck Injuries

There is a very wide range of neck injuries. Many are found in conjunction with back and shoulder problems. At the very bottom end of neck and back injuries, further guidance may be obtained from the Minor Injuries chapter in the Guidelines.

(a) Severe

		In the region of £126,550	with 10% uplift In the region of £139,210

(i) Neck injury associated with incomplete paraplegia or resulting in permanent spastic quadriparesis or where the injured person, despite wearing a collar 24 hours a day for a period of years, still has little or no movement in the neck and suffers severe headaches which have proved intractable.

In the region of £126,550 — *In the region of £139,210*

(ii) Injuries, usually involving serious fractures or damage to discs in the cervical spine, which give rise to disabilities which fall short of those in (a)(i) above but which are of considerable severity; for example, permanent damage to the brachial plexus or substantial loss of movement in the neck and loss of function in one or more limbs.

£56,100 to £111,690 — *£61,710 to £122,860*

(iii) Injuries causing fractures or dislocations or severe damage to soft tissues and/or ruptured tendons that lead to chronic conditions and significant disability of a permanent nature. The precise award depends on the length of time during which the most serious symptoms are ameliorated, the extent of the treatment required, and on the prognosis.

£38,800 to £47,760 — *£42,680 to £52,540*

(b) Moderate

(i) Injuries such as fractures or dislocations which cause severe immediate symptoms and which may necessitate spinal fusion. This bracket will also include chronic conditions, usually involving referred symptoms to other parts of the anatomy or serious soft tissue injuries to the neck and back combined. They leave markedly

£21,320 to £32,840 — *£23,460 to £36,120*

impaired function or vulnerability to further trauma, and limitation of activities. Depending on severity of injury this bracket can include cases where there are pre-existing degenerative changes or where symptoms have been accelerated.

		with 10% uplift

(ii) Cases involving soft tissue or wrenching-type injury and disc lesion of the more severe type resulting in cervical spondylosis, serious limitation of movement, permanent or recurring pain, stiffness or discomfort, and the possible need for further surgery or increased vulnerability to further trauma. This bracket will also include injuries which may have accelerated and/or exacerbated a pre-existing condition over a prolonged period of time, usually by five years or more.

£11,730 to £21,320 — **£12,900 to £23,460**

(iii) Injuries which may have accelerated and/or exacerbated a pre-existing condition over a shorter period of time, usually less than five years. This bracket will also apply to moderate soft tissue injuries where the period of recovery has been fairly protracted and where there remains an increased vulnerability to further trauma or permanent nuisance type symptoms referring from the neck.

£6,730 to £11,730 — **£7,410 to £12,900**

(c) Minor

This bracket includes minor soft tissue injuries. Whilst the duration of symptoms will always be important, factors such as those listed below may justify an award in either a higher or lower bracket.

- the severity of the neck injury;
- the intensity of pain experienced and the consistency of symptoms;
- the extent to which ongoing symptoms are of a minor nature only;
- the presence of additional symptoms in the back and/or shoulder and/or referred headaches;
- the impact of the symptoms on the injured person's ability to function in everyday life and engage in social/recreational activities;
- the impact of the injuries on the injured person's ability to work;
- the extent of any treatment required;
- the need to take medication to control symptoms of pain and discomfort.

		with 10% uplift
(i) Where a full recovery takes place within a period of about one to two years. This bracket will also apply to short-term acceleration and/or exacerbation injuries, usually between one and two years.	£3,710 to £6,730	£4,080 to £7,410
(ii) Where a full recovery takes place between three months and a year. This bracket will also apply to very short-term acceleration and/or exacerbation injuries, usually less than one year.	£2,090 to £3,710	£2,300 to £4,080
(iii) Where a full recovery is made within three months.	Up to £2,090	Up to £2,300

(B) Back Injuries

(a) Severe

		with 10% uplift

(i) Cases of the most severe injury involving damage to the spinal cord and nerve roots, leading to a combination of very serious consequences not normally found in cases of back injury. There will be severe pain and disability with a combination of incomplete paralysis and significantly impaired bladder, bowel, and sexual function.

£77,700 to £137,330

£85,470 to £151,070

(ii) Cases which have special features taking them outside any lower bracket applicable to orthopaedic injury to the back. Such features include nerve root damage with associated loss of sensation, impaired mobility, impaired bladder and bowel function, sexual difficulties, and unsightly scarring.

£63,280 to £75,440

£69,600 to £82,980

(iii) Cases of disc lesions or fractures of discs or of vertebral bodies or soft tissue injuries leading to chronic conditions where, despite treatment (usually involving surgery), there remain disabilities such as continuing severe pain and discomfort, impaired agility, impaired sexual function, depression, personality change, alcoholism, unemployability, and the risk of arthritis.

£33,080 to £59,490

£36,390 to £65,440

(b) Moderate

with 10% uplift

(i) Cases where any residual disability is of less severity than that in (a)(iii) above. The bracket contains a wide variety of injuries. Examples are a case of a compression/crush fracture of the lumbar vertebrae where there is a substantial risk of osteoarthritis and constant pain and discomfort; that of a traumatic spondylolisthesis with continuous pain and a probability that spinal fusion will be necessary; a prolapsed intervertebral disc requiring surgery; or damage to an intervertebral disc with nerve root irritation and reduced mobility.

£23,680 to £33,080   £26,050 to £36,390

(ii) Many frequently encountered injuries to the back such as disturbance of ligaments and muscles giving rise to backache, soft tissue injuries resulting in a prolonged acceleration and/or exacerbation of a pre-existing back condition, usually by five years or more, or prolapsed discs necessitating laminectomy or resulting in repeated relapses. The precise figure will depend upon a number of factors including the severity of the original injury, the degree of pain experienced, the extent of any treatment required in the past or in the future, the impact of the symptoms on the injured person's ability to function in everyday life and engage in social/recreational activities and the prognosis for the future.

£10,670 to £23,680   £11,730 to £26,050

(c) Minor

This bracket includes less serious strains, sprains, disc prolapses, soft tissue injuries, or fracture injuries which recover without surgery. As with minor neck injuries, whilst the duration of symptoms will always be important, factors such as those listed below may justify an award in either a higher or lower bracket.

- the severity of the original injury;
- the degree of pain experienced and the consistency of symptoms;
- the extent to which ongoing symptoms are of a minor nature only;
- the presence of any additional symptoms in other parts of the anatomy, particularly the neck;
- the impact of the symptoms on the injured person's ability to function in everyday life and engage in social/recreational activities;
- the impact of the injuries on the injured person's ability to work;
- the extent of any treatment required;
- the need to take medication to control symptoms of pain and discomfort.

		with 10% uplift
(i) Where a full recovery or a recovery to nuisance level takes place without surgery within about two to five years. This bracket will also apply to shorter term acceleration and/or exacerbation injuries, usually between two to five years.	£6,730 to £10,670	£7,410 to £11,730

		with 10% uplift

(ii) Where a full recovery takes place without surgery between three months and two years. This bracket will also apply to very short-term acceleration and/or exacerbation injuries, usually less than two years. — £2,090 to £6,730 — **£2,300 to £7,410**

(iii) Where a full recovery is made within three months. — Up to £2,090 — **Up to £2,300**

(C) Shoulder Injuries

(a) Severe — £16,380 to £40,970 — **£18,020 to £45,070**

Often associated with neck injuries and involving damage to the brachial plexus (see (A)(a)(ii)) resulting in significant disability. Serious brachial plexus injuries causing significant neck and/or arm symptoms should be assessed under brackets (A)(a)(ii) or (F)(a).

(b) Serious — £10,890 to £16,380 — **£11,980 to £18,020**

Dislocation of the shoulder and damage to the lower part of the brachial plexus causing pain in shoulder and neck, aching in elbow, sensory symptoms in the forearm and hand, and weakness of grip or a fractured humerus leading to restricted shoulder movement. Cases of rotator cuff injury with persisting symptoms after surgery will usually fall within this bracket, as will cases of soft tissue injury where intrusive symptoms will be permanent.

		with 10% uplift
(c) Moderate	£6,730 to £10,890	**£7,410 to £11,980**

Frozen shoulder with limitation of movement and discomfort with symptoms persisting for about two years. Also soft tissue injuries with more than minimal symptoms persisting after two years but not permanent.

(d) Minor

Soft tissue injury to shoulder with considerable pain but almost complete recovery:

The starting point for the assessment will be the duration of symptoms but the severity of the original injury, the degree of pain experienced, and the extent to which ongoing symptoms are of a minor nature only may justify an award in a higher or lower bracket.

(i) in less than two years;	£3,710 to £6,730	**£4,080 to £7,410**
(ii) within a year;	£2,090 to £3,710	**£2,300 to £4,080**
(iii) within three months.	Up to £2,090	**Up to £2,300**

(e) Fracture of Clavicle	£4,390 to £10,440	**£4,830 to £11,490**

The level of the award will depend on extent of fracture, level of disability, residual symptoms, whether temporary or permanent, and whether union is anatomically displaced. Unusually serious cases may exceed this bracket and regard may be had to bracket (C)(b) above.

(D) Injuries to the Pelvis and Hips

The most serious of injuries to the pelvis and hip can be as devastating as a leg amputation and accordingly will attract a similar award of damages.

(a) Severe

		with 10% uplift
(i) Extensive fractures of the pelvis involving, for example, dislocation of a low back joint and a ruptured bladder, or a hip injury resulting in spondylolisthesis of a low back joint with intolerable pain and necessitating spinal fusion. Inevitably there will be substantial residual disabilities such as a complicated arthrodesis with resulting lack of bladder and bowel control, sexual dysfunction, or hip deformity making the use of a calliper essential; or may present difficulties for natural delivery.	£66,890 to £111,690	£73,580 to £122,860
(ii) Injuries only a little less severe than in (a)(i) above but with particular distinguishing features lifting them above any lower bracket. Examples are: (a) fracture dislocation of the pelvis involving both ischial and pubic rami and resulting in impotence; or (b) traumatic myositis ossificans with formation of ectopic bone around the hip.	£52,810 to £66,890	£58,100 to £73,580
(iii) Many injuries fall within this bracket: a fracture of the acetabulum leading to degenerative changes and leg instability requiring an osteotomy and the likelihood of hip replacement surgery in the future; the fracture of an	£33,430 to £44,790	£36,770 to £49,270

arthritic femur or hip necessitating hip replacement; or a fracture resulting in a hip replacement which is only partially successful so that there is a clear risk of the need for revision surgery.

(b) Moderate

		with 10% uplift
(i) Significant injury to the pelvis or hip but any permanent disability is not major and any future risk not great.	£22,680 to £33,430	£24,950 to £36,770
(ii) These cases may involve hip replacement or other surgery. Where it has been carried out wholly successfully the award will tend to the top of the bracket, but the bracket also includes cases where hip replacement may be necessary in the foreseeable future or where there are more than minimal ongoing symptoms.	£10,750 to £22,680	£11,820 to £24,950

(c) Lesser Injuries

(i) Cases where despite significant injury there is little or no residual disability. Where there has been a complete recovery within two years, the award may but is unlikely to exceed the mid-point in the range.	£3,370 to £10,750	£3,710 to £11,820
(ii) Minor soft tissue injuries with complete recovery.	Up to £3,370	Up to £3,710

(E) Amputation of Arms

The value of any amputation injury depends upon:

(i) whether the amputation is above or below the elbow. The loss of the additional joint adds greatly to the disability;

(ii) the extent to which prosthetics can restore function;

(iii) whether or not the amputation was of the dominant arm;

(iv) the intensity of any phantom pains;

(v) the claimant's age;

(vi) the effect on work, domestic, and social life.

		with 10% uplift
(a) Loss of Both Arms	£205,420 to £255,930	£225,960 to £281,520

The effect of such an injury is to reduce a person with full awareness to a state of considerable helplessness.

(b) Loss of One Arm		
(i) Arm Amputated at the Shoulder	Not less than £117,010	Not less than £128,710
(ii) Above-elbow Amputation	£93,540 to £111,690	£102,890 to £122,860

A shorter stump may create difficulties in the use of a prosthesis. This will make the level of the award towards the top end of the bracket. Amputation through the elbow will normally produce an award at the bottom end of the bracket.

		with 10% uplift
(iii) Below-elbow Amputation	£82,040 to £93,540	£90,250 to £102,890

Amputation through the forearm with residual severe organic and phantom pains would attract an award at the top end of the bracket.

(F) Other Arm Injuries

(a) Severe Injuries	£82,040 to £111,690	£90,250 to £122,860

Injuries which fall short of amputation but which are extremely serious and leave the injured person little better off than if the arm had been lost; for example, a serious brachial plexus injury.

(b) Injuries Resulting in Permanent and Substantial Disablement	£33,430 to £51,070	£36,770 to £56,180

Serious fractures of one or both forearms where there is significant permanent residual disability whether functional or cosmetic.

(c) Less Severe Injury	£16,380 to £33,430	£18,020 to £36,770

While there will have been significant disabilities, a substantial degree of recovery will have taken place or will be expected.

		with 10% uplift
(d) Simple Fractures of the Forearm	£5,630 to £16,380	£6,190 to £18,020

(G) Injuries to the Elbow

(a) A Severely Disabling Injury	£33,430 to £46,780	£36,770 to £51,460
(b) Less Severe Injuries	£13,360 to £27,320	£14,690 to £30,050

Injuries causing impairment of function but not involving major surgery or significant disability.

(c) Moderate or Minor Injury	Up to £10,750	Up to £11,820

Most elbow injuries fall into this category. They comprise simple fractures, tennis elbow syndrome, and lacerations; i.e., those injuries which cause no permanent damage and do not result in any permanent impairment of function.

(i) Injuries fully resolving after about one year will usually attract an award in the region of £3,010 (**£3,310** accounting for 10% uplift).

(ii) Injuries with the majority of symptoms resolving within 18 to 24 months but with nuisance level symptoms persisting after that would attract an award of £5,360 (**£5,890** accounting for 10% uplift).

(iii) Injuries recovering after three years with nuisance symptoms thereafter and/or requiring surgery will attract awards towards the top of the bracket.

(H) Wrist Injuries

			with 10% uplift
(a)	Injuries resulting in complete loss of function in the wrist, for example, where an arthrodesis has been performed.	£40,630 to £51,070	£44,690 to £56,180
(b)	Injury resulting in significant permanent disability, but where some useful movement remains.	£20,900 to £33,430	£22,990 to £36,770
(c)	Less severe injuries where these still result in some permanent disability as, for example, a degree of persisting pain and stiffness.	£10,750 to £20,900	£11,820 to £22,990
(d)	Where recovery from fracture or soft tissue injury takes longer but is complete, the award will rarely exceed £8,740 (**£9,620** with 10% uplift).	Rarely exceed £8,740	Rarely exceed £9,620
(e)	An uncomplicated Colles' fracture.	In the region of £6,340	In the region of £6,970
(f)	Very minor undisplaced or minimally displaced fractures and soft tissue injuries necessitating application of plaster or bandage for a matter of weeks and a full or virtual recovery within up to 12 months or so.	£3,010 to £4,050	£3,310 to £4,450

(I) Hand Injuries

The hands are cosmetically and functionally the most important component parts of the upper limbs. The loss of a hand is valued not far short of the amount which would be awarded for the loss of the arm itself. The upper end of any bracket will generally be appropriate where the injury is to the dominant hand.

In cases of injuries to multiple digits, practitioners and judges should not simply add the figures which would be appropriate for each injury separately, but should consider the overall extent of pain, suffering, and loss of amenity, usually leading to a lower award than would be appropriate by simple addition.

			with 10% uplift
(a)	Total or Effective Loss of Both Hands	£120,040 to £171,920	£132,040 to £189,110

Serious injury resulting in extensive damage to both hands such as to render them little more than useless. The top of the bracket is applicable where no effective prosthesis can be used.

(b)	Serious Damage to Both Hands	£47,550 to £72,150	£52,310 to £79,360

Such injuries will have given rise to permanent cosmetic disability and significant loss of function.

(c)	Total or Effective Loss of One Hand	£82,040 to £93,540	£90,250 to £102,890

This bracket will apply to a hand which was crushed and thereafter surgically amputated or where all fingers and most of the palm have been traumatically amputated. The upper end of the bracket is indicated where the hand so damaged was the dominant one.

(d)	Amputation of Index and Middle and/or Ring Fingers	£52,810 to £77,430	£58,100 to £85,170

The hand will have been rendered of very little use and such grip as remains will be exceedingly weak.

		with 10% uplift

(e) Serious Hand Injuries — £24,740 to £52,810 | **£27,220 to £58,100**

Such injuries will, for example, have reduced the hand to about 50 per cent capacity. Included would be cases where several fingers have been amputated but rejoined to the hand leaving it clawed, clumsy, and unsightly, or amputation of some fingers together with part of the palm resulting in gross diminution of grip and dexterity and gross cosmetic disfigurement.

(f) Severe Fractures to Fingers — Up to £31,350 | **Up to £34,480**

These may lead to partial amputations and result in deformity, impairment of grip, reduced mechanical function, and disturbed sensation.

(g) Less Serious Hand Injury — £12,340 to £24,740 | **£13,570 to £27,220**

Such as a severe crush injury resulting in significantly impaired function without future surgery or despite operative treatment undergone.

(h) Moderate Hand Injury — £4,780 to £11,330 | **£5,260 to £12,460**

Crush injuries, penetrating wounds, soft tissue type and deep lacerations. The top of the bracket would be appropriate where surgery has failed and permanent disability remains. The bottom of the bracket would be appropriate for permanent but non-intrusive symptoms.

(i) Total and Partial Loss of Index Finger — £10,380 to £15,990 | **£11,420 to £17,590**

53

Total loss will likely result in an award at the top end of the bracket.

This bracket also covers cases of injury to the index finger giving rise to disfigurement and impairment of grip or dexterity.

		with 10% uplift
(j) Fracture of Index Finger	£7,780 to £10,440	£8,550 to £11,480

This level is appropriate where a fracture has mended quickly but grip has remained impaired, there is pain on heavy use, and osteoarthritis is likely in due course.

(k) Serious Injury to Ring or Middle Fingers	£12,700 to £13,940	£13,970 to £15,330

Fractures or serious injury to tendons causing stiffness, deformity, and permanent loss of grip or dexterity will fall within this bracket. This bracket will include awards for total loss of middle finger.

(l) Loss of the Terminal Phalanx of the Ring or Middle Fingers	£3,370 to £6,720	£3,710 to £7,390
(m) Amputation of Little Finger	£7,380 to £10,440	£8,110 to £11,490
(n) Loss of Part of the Little Finger	£3,370 to £5,000	£3,710 to £5,500

This is appropriate where the remaining tip is sensitive.

(o) Amputation of Ring and Little Fingers	In the region of £18,620	In the region of £20,480

			with 10% uplift
(p)	Amputation of the Terminal Phalanges of the Index and Middle Fingers	In the region of £21,320	In the region of £23,460

Such injury will involve scarring, restriction of movement, and impairment of grip and fine handling.

(q)	Loss of Thumb	£30,300 to £46,780	£33,330 to £51,460

(r)	Very Serious Injury to Thumb	£16,720 to £29,860	£18,390 to £32,850

This bracket is appropriate where the thumb has been severed at the base and grafted back leaving a virtually useless and de-formed digit, or where the thumb has been amputated through the interphalangeal joint.

(s)	Serious Injury to the Thumb	£10,750 to £14,310	£11,820 to £15,740

Such injuries may involve amputation of the tip, nerve damage or fracture necessitating the insertion of wires as a result of which the thumb is cold and ultra-sensitive and there is impaired grip and loss of manual dexterity.

(t)	Moderate Injuries to the Thumb	£8,250 to £10,750	£9,080 to £11,820

These are injuries such as those necessitating arthrodesis of the interphalangeal joint or causing damage to tendons or nerves. Such injuries result in impairment of sensation and function and cosmetic deformity.

		with 10% uplift
(u) Severe Dislocation of the Thumb	£3,370 to £5,790	£3,710 to £6,360
(v) Minor Hand, Finger and Thumb Injuries	Up to £4,055	Up to £4,461

This will include fractures which generally have recovered in six months. Also injuries such as scarring, tenderness, and reaction to the cold where there is full recovery.

(J) Vibration White Finger (VWF) and/or Hand Arm Vibration Syndrome (HAVS)

Vibration White Finger and/or Hand Arm Vibration Syndrome, caused by exposure to vibration, is a slowly progressive condition, the development and severity of which are affected by the degree of exposure, in particular the magnitude, frequency, duration, and transmission of the vibration. The symptoms are similar to those experienced in the constitutional condition of Raynaud's phenomenon.

The Stockholm Workshop Scale is now the accepted table for medical grading of the severity of the condition. The Scale classifies both the vascular and sensorineural components in two complementary tables. Individual assessment is made separately for each hand and for each finger.

The vascular component is graded between Stage 0V (no attacks) through mild, moderate, and severe to 4V (very severe) where there are frequent attacks affecting all phalanges of most fingers with atrophic changes in the fingertips. The sensorineural component is graded between Stage 0SN (no symptoms) and 3SN (intermittent or persistent numbness, reduced tactile discrimination, and/or manipulative dexterity). The grade of disorder is indicated by the stage and number of affected fingers on both hands.

Any interference with work or social life is disregarded in that grading.

The assessment of damages is therefore not strictly tied to the Stockholm Workshop Scale grading. It depends more on the extent of the symptoms and their impact, having regard to the following factors:

(i) age at onset;

(ii) whether one or both hands are affected and, if only one, whether it is the dominant hand;

(iii) number of fingers affected;

(iv) extent of impaired dexterity and/or reduction in grip strength;

(v) frequency and duration of painful episodes;

(vi) effect of symptoms on work, domestic, and social life.

Accordingly, depending on individual circumstances, a lower award might be made despite significant Stockholm Workshop Scale grading where, e.g., employment is unaffected, whilst a higher award might be attracted where there is a lesser grading but a greater impact on normal life.

In a severe case, the injury may be regarded as damaging a hand rather than being confined to the fingers.

The brackets can best be defined and valued as follows (note that it is not intended that these should correlate directly with the Stockholm Workshop Scale):

		with 10% uplift
(a) Most Serious	£26,990 to £32,780	**£29,690 to £36,060**

Persisting bilateral symptoms in a younger person which interfere significantly with daily life and lead to a change in employment.

(b) Serious	£14,310 to £26,990	**£15,740 to £29,690**

In this bracket there will have been a marked interference with work and domestic activity. Attacks may occur throughout the year.

(c) Moderate	£7,380 to £14,310	**£8,110 to £15,740**

This bracket will include claimants in their middle years where employment has been maintained or varied only to remove excess vibration. Attacks will occur mostly in cold weather.

	with 10% uplift
£2,560 to £7,380	£2,810 to £8,110

(d) Minor

Occasional symptoms in only a few fingers with a modest effect on work or leisure.

(K) Work-related Upper Limb Disorders

This section covers a range of upper limb injury in the form of the following pathological conditions:

(a) Tenosynovitis: inflammation of synovial sheaths of tendons usually resolving with rest over a short period. Sometimes this condition leads to continuing symptoms of loss of grip and dexterity.

(b) De Quervain's tenosynovitis: a form of tenosynovitis, rarely bilateral, involving inflammation of the tendons of the thumb.

(c) Stenosing tenosynovitis: otherwise, trigger finger/thumb: thickening tendons.

(d) Carpal tunnel syndrome: constriction of the median nerve of the wrist or thickening of surrounding tissue. It is often relieved by a decompression operation.

(e) Epicondylitis: inflammation in the elbow joint: medial = golfer's elbow; lateral = tennis elbow. The brackets below apply to all these conditions but the level of the award is affected by the following considerations regardless of the precise condition:

    (i) are the effects bilateral or one-sided (and, if one-sided, whether it is the dominant hand)?

    (ii) the level of symptoms, i.e., pain, swelling, tenderness, crepitus;

    (iii) the ability to work and the effect on domestic and social life;

    (iv) the capacity to avoid the recurrence of symptoms;

    (v) surgery;

    (vi) age;

    (vii) which, if any, of the symptoms would have been suffered in any event and when.

			with 10% uplift
(a)	Continuing bilateral disability with surgery and loss of employment.	£18,690 to £19,730	£20,560 to £21,700
(b)	Continuing, but fluctuating and unilateral symptoms.	£12,700 to £13,940	£13,970 to £15,330
(c)	Symptoms resolving in the course of up to three years.	£7,380 to £9,170	£8,110 to £10,090

		with 10% uplift
(d) Complete recovery within a short period (of weeks or a few months).	£1,880 to £3,010	£2,070 to £3,310

(L) Leg Injuries

(a) Amputations

(i) Loss of Both Legs — £205,420 to £240,590 — £225,960 to £264,650

This is the appropriate award where both legs are lost above the knee or one leg has been lost above the knee at a high level and the other leg has been lost below the knee. The level of award will be determined by factors such as the severity of any phantom pains; associated psychological problems; the success of any prosthetics; any side effects such as backache; and the risk of future degenerative changes in the hips and spine.

(ii) Below-knee Amputation of Both Legs — £171,920 to £230,440 — £189,110 to £253,480

The level of the amputations will be important, with an award at the top of the bracket appropriate where both legs are amputated just below the knee. Otherwise, the award will depend upon factors such as the severity of any phantom pains; associated psychological problems; the success of any prosthetics; any side effects such as backache; and the risk of developing degenerative changes in the remaining joints of both lower limbs or in the hips and spine.

		with 10% uplift
(iii) Above-knee Amputation of One Leg	£89,440 to £117,280	£98,380 to £129,010

The award will depend upon such factors as the level of the amputation; the severity of any phantom pains; associated psychological problems; the success of any prosthetics; any side effects such as backache; and the risk of developing osteoarthritis in the remaining joints of both lower limbs or in the hips and spine.

(iv) Below-knee Amputation of One Leg	£83,590 to £113,450	£91,950 to £124,800

The straightforward case of a below-knee amputation with no complications would justify an award towards the bottom of this bracket. At or towards the top of the range would come the traumatic amputation which occurs in a devastating accident, where the injured person remained fully conscious, or cases where attempts to save the leg led to numerous unsuccessful operations so that amputation occurred years after the event. Factors such as phantom pains, the success of any prosthetics, associated psychological problems, and the increased chance of developing osteoarthritis in the remaining joints of both limbs will also be important in determining the appropriate award.

(b) Severe Leg Injuries

(i) The Most Serious Injuries Short of Amputation	£82,110 to £115,940	£90,320 to £127,530

Some injuries, although not involving amputation, are so severe that the courts have awarded damages at a similar level. Such injuries would include extensive degloving of the leg, where there is gross shortening of the leg, or where fractures have not united and extensive bone grafting has been undertaken.

			with 10% uplift
(ii)	Very Serious	£46,780 to £77,040	£51,460 to £85,600

Injuries leading to permanent problems with mobility, the need for crutches or mobility aids for the remainder of the injured person's life; injuries where multiple fractures have taken years to heal, required extensive treatment, and have led to serious deformity and limitation of movement, or where arthritis has developed in a joint so that further surgical treatment is likely.

(iii)	Serious	£33,450 to £46,780	£36,790 to £51,460

Serious compound or comminuted fractures or injuries to joints or ligaments resulting in instability, prolonged treatment, a lengthy period of non-weight-bearing, the near certainty that arthritis will ensue; extensive scarring. To justify an award within this bracket a combination of such features will generally be necessary.

(iv)	Moderate	£23,680 to £33,450	£26,050 to £36,790

This bracket includes complicated or multiple fractures or severe crushing injuries, generally to a single limb. The level of an award within the bracket will be influenced by the extent of treatment undertaken; impact on employment; the presence or risk of degenerative changes and/or future surgery; imperfect union of fractures; muscle wasting; limited joint movements; instability in the knee; unsightly scarring; or permanently increased vulnerability to future damage.

(c) Less Serious Leg Injuries

			with 10% uplift
(i)	Fractures from which an Incomplete Recovery is Made or Serious Soft Tissue Injuries	£15,320 to £23,680	£16,860 to £26,050

In the case of fracture injuries, the injured person will have made a reasonable recovery but will be left with a metal implant and/or defective gait, a limp, impaired mobility, sensory loss, discomfort or an exacerbation of a pre-existing disability. This bracket will also involve serious soft tissue injuries to one or both legs causing significant cosmetic deficit, functional restriction and/or some nerve damage in the lower limbs.

(ii)	Simple Fracture of a Femur with No Damage to Articular Surfaces	£7,780 to £12,010	£8,550 to £13,210
(iii)	Simple Fractures to Tibia or Fibula or Soft Tissue Injuries	Up to £10,100	Up to £11,110

Towards the top of the bracket there will come simple fractures of the tibia or fibula where there are some ongoing minor symptoms such as dull aching and/or modest restriction of movement. Where there has been a simple fracture of the tibia or fibula with a complete recovery, an award of less than £7,770 (**£8,550** accounting for 10% uplift) is likely to be justified. The level of award will be influenced by time spent in plaster and the length of the recovery period. Below this level fall a wide variety of soft tissue injuries, lacerations, cuts, bruising, or contusions, all of which have recovered completely or almost so and any residual disability is cosmetic or of a minor nature. Where these modest injuries have fully resolved within a few months an award of less than £2,090 (**£2,300** accounting for 10% uplift) is likely to be justified.

(M) Knee Injuries

(a)   Severe

		with 10% uplift
(i)	Serious knee injury where there has been disruption of the joint, the development of osteoarthritis, gross ligamentous damage, lengthy treatment, considerable pain and loss of function, and an arthroplasty or arthrodesis has taken place or is inevitable.	£59,490 to £82,080	**£65,440** **to £90,290**
(ii)	Leg fracture extending into the knee joint causing pain which is constant, permanent, limiting movement or impairing agility, and rendering the injured person prone to osteoarthritis and at risk of arthroplasty.	£44,470 to £59,490	**£48,920** **to £65,440**

			with 10% uplift

(iii) Less severe injuries than those in (a) (ii) above and/or injuries which result in less severe disability. There may be continuing symptoms by way of pain and discomfort and limitation of movement or instability or deformity with the risk that degenerative changes and the need for remedial surgery may occur in the long term as a result of damage to the kneecap, ligamentous or meniscal injury, or muscular wasting.

£22,340 to £37,070 — **£24,580 to £40,770**

(b) Moderate

(i) Injuries involving dislocation, torn cartilage or meniscus which results in minor instability, wasting, weakness, or other mild future disability. This bracket also includes injuries which accelerate symptoms from a pre-existing condition over a prolonged period of years.

£12,650 to £22,340 — **£13,920 to £24,580**

(ii) This bracket includes injuries similar to those in (b)(i) above, but less serious and involving shorter periods of acceleration or exacerbation, and also lacerations, twisting, or bruising injuries. Where there is continuous aching or discomfort, or occasional pain, the award will be towards the upper end of the bracket. Where recovery has been complete or almost complete the award is unlikely to exceed £5,160 (**£5,680** accounting for 10% uplift). Modest injuries that resolve within a short space of time will attract lower awards.

Up to £11,730 — **Up to £12,900**

(N) Ankle Injuries

with 10% uplift

(a) Very Severe

£42,710 to £59,480 — **£46,980 to £65,420**

Examples of injuries falling within this bracket are limited and unusual. They include cases of a transmalleolar fracture of the ankle with extensive soft-tissue damage resulting in deformity and the risk that any future injury to the leg might necessitate a below-knee amputation, or cases of bilateral ankle fractures causing degeneration of the joints at a young age so that arthrodesis is necessary.

(b) Severe

£26,710 to £42,710 — **£29,380 to £46,980**

Injuries necessitating an extensive period of treatment and/or a lengthy period in plaster or where pins and plates have been inserted and there is significant residual disability in the form of ankle instability and severely limited ability to walk. The level of the award within the bracket will be determined in part by such features as a failed arthrodesis, the presence of or risk of osteoarthritis, regular sleep disturbance, unsightly scarring, impact on employment, and any need to wear special footwear.

(c) Moderate

£11,730 to £22,680 — **£12,900 to £24,950**

Fractures, ligamentous tears and the like which give rise to less serious disabilities such as difficulty in walking on uneven ground, difficulty standing or walking for long periods of time, awkwardness on stairs, irritation from metal plates, and residual scarring. There may also be a risk of future osteoarthritis.

		with 10% uplift

(d) Modest Injuries

Up to £11,730 — Up to **£12,900**

The less serious, minor or undisplaced fractures, sprains, and ligamentous injuries. The level of the award within the bracket will be determined by whether or not a complete recovery has been made and, if recovery is incomplete, whether there is any tendency for the ankle to give way, and whether there is scarring, aching or discomfort, loss of movement, or the possibility of long-term osteoarthritis.

Where recovery is complete without any ongoing symptoms or scarring, the award is unlikely to exceed £6,560 (**£7,220** accounting for 10% uplift). Where recovery is complete within a year, the award is unlikely to exceed £4,690 (**£5,160** accounting for 10% uplift). Modest injuries that resolve within a short space of time will attract lower awards.

(O) Achilles Tendon

(a) Most Serious

In the region of £32,780 — **In the region of £36,060**

Severance of the tendon and the peroneus longus muscle giving rise to cramp, swelling, and restricted ankle movement necessitating the cessation of active sports.

		with 10% uplift

(b) Serious

£21,320 to £25,670

£23,460 to £28,240

Where complete division of the tendon has been successfully repaired but there is residual weakness, a limitation of ankle movements, a limp, and residual scarring and where further improvement is unlikely.

(c) Moderate

£10,750 to £17,970

£11,820 to £19,770

Cases involving partial rupture or significant injury to the tendon. The level of award within the bracket will be determined by the treatment received (whether conservative or invasive), the level of recovery made, ongoing pain, any continuing functional disability, and permanent scarring.

(d) Minor

£6,200 to £10,750

£6,820 to £11,820

A turning of the ankle resulting in some damage to the tendon and a feeling of being unsure of ankle support would fall within this bracket. The consequences of these injuries may be similar to modest ankle injuries and further guidance may be obtained from bracket (N)(d).

(P) Foot Injuries

(a) Amputation of Both Feet

£144,520 to £171,920

£158,970 to £189,110

This injury is treated similarly to below-knee amputation of both legs because the common feature is loss of a useful ankle joint.

		with 10% uplift

(b) Amputation of One Foot

£71,640 to £93,540   **£78,800 to £102,890**

This injury is also treated as similar to a below-knee amputation because of the loss of the ankle joint.

(c) Very Severe

£71,640 to £93,540   **£78,800 to £102,890**

To fall within this bracket the injury must produce permanent and severe pain or really serious permanent disability. Examples would include the traumatic amputation of the forefoot where there was a significant risk of the need for a full amputation and serious exacerbation of an existing back problem, or cases of the loss of a substantial portion of the heel so that mobility was grossly restricted.

(d) Severe

£35,810 to £59,730   **£39,390 to £65,710**

Fractures of *both* heels or feet with a substantial restriction on mobility or considerable and permanent pain. The bracket will also include unusually severe injury to a single foot. Examples include injuries that result in severe degloving, extensive surgery, heel fusion, osteoporosis, ulceration, or other disability preventing the wearing of ordinary shoes. It will also apply in the case of a drop foot deformity corrected by a brace.

(e) Serious

£21,320 to £33,450   **£23,460 to £36,790**

This bracket will include injuries less severe than in (d) above but leading to continuing pain from traumatic arthritis or the risk of future arthritis, prolonged treatment and the risk of fusion surgery.

			with 10% uplift

(f) **Moderate**

Displaced metatarsal fractures resulting in permanent deformity and continuing symptoms. There may be a risk of long-term osteoarthritis and/or future surgery.

£11,730 to £21,320 — **£12,900 to £23,460**

(g) **Modest**

Simple metatarsal fractures, ruptured ligaments, puncture wounds and the like. Where there are continuing symptoms, such as a permanent limp, pain, or aching, awards between £5,980 (**£6,580** accounting for 10% uplift) and £11,730 (**£12,900** accounting for 10% uplift) would be appropriate. Straightforward foot injuries such as fractures, lacerations, contusions etc. from which complete or near complete recovery is made would justify awards of £5,980 (**£6,580** accounting for 10% uplift) or less. Modest inpjuries that resolve within a short space of time will attract lower awards. Awards for minor foot injuries resolving within a few months, with little impact on lifestyle or day to day activities, are unlikely to exceed £2,090 (**£2,300** accounting for 10% uplift).

Up to £11,730 — **Up to £12,900**

(Q) Toe Injuries

(a) **Amputation of All Toes**

The position within the bracket will be determined by, for example, whether or not the amputation was traumatic or surgical and the extent of the loss of the forefoot together with the residual effects on mobility.

£31,150 to £47,830 — **£34,270 to £52,620**

		with 10% uplift
(b) Amputation of the Great Toe	In the region of £26,710	**In the region of £29,380**
(c) Severe Toe Injuries	£11,730 to £17,970	**£12,900 to £29,770**

This is the appropriate bracket for severe crush injuries, leading to amputation of one or two toes (other than the great toe) or falling short of the need for amputation or necessitating only partial amputation. It also includes bursting wounds and injuries resulting in severe damage and in any event producing significant continuing symptoms.

(d) Serious Toe Injuries	£8,190 to £11,730	**£9,010 to £12,900**

Such injuries will be serious injuries to the great toe or crush and multiple fractures of two or more toes. There will be some permanent disability by way of discomfort, pain, or sensitive scarring to justify an award within this bracket. Where there have been a number of unsuccessful operations or persisting stabbing pains, impaired gait or the like the award will tend towards the top end of the bracket.

(e) Moderate Toe Injuries	Up to £8,190	**Up to £9,010**

These injuries include relatively straightforward fractures or the exacerbation of a pre-existing degenerative condition or laceration injuries to one or more toes. Cases involving prolonged minor symptoms and/or the need for surgery resulting in prolonged discomfort and permanent scarring are likely to justify awards towards the upper end of this bracket. Only £4,770 (**£5,250** accounting for 10% uplift) or less would be awarded for straightforward fractures or crushing/soft tissue injuries of one or more toes with complete resolution or near complete resolution. Modest injuries that resolve within a short space of time will attract lower awards.

8

Chronic Pain

This chapter deals with a variety of what may loosely be described as 'pain disorders'. This includes Fibromyalgia, Chronic Pain Syndrome, Chronic Fatigue Syndrome (also known as ME), Conversion Disorders (also known as Dissociative Disorders), and Somatic Symptom Disorders. Many such disorders are characterized by subjective pain without any, or any commensurate, organic basis. The figures given here assume causation of relevant symptoms is established. Cases of short-lived pain disorders, short-term exacerbation of an existing pain disorder, or brief acceleration of the onset of a pain disorder, all fall outside the suggested brackets and will require separate consideration.

With the exception of cases of Complex Regional Pain Syndrome (also known as CRPS), no attempt has been made to sub-divide between different clinical conditions. Guidance instead reflects the impact, severity, and prognosis of the condition. Where the condition principally affects a single part of the anatomy, cross-reference to the relevant chapter within the Judicial College Guidelines may assist. The presence of an overlapping psychiatric injury is commonplace in such cases.

The factors to be taken into account in valuing claims for pain disorders (including CRPS) include the following:

(i) the degree of pain experienced;

(ii) the overall impact of the symptoms (which may include fatigue, associated impairments of cognitive function, muscle weakness, headaches etc. and taking account of any fluctuation in symptoms) on mobility, ability to function in daily life, and the need for care/assistance;

(iii) the effect of the condition on the injured person's ability to work;

(iv) the need to take medication to control symptoms of pain and the effect of such medication on the person's ability to function in normal daily life;

(v) the extent to which treatment has been undertaken and its effect (or its predicted effect in respect of future treatment);

(vi) whether the condition is limited to one anatomical site or is widespread;

(vii) the presence of any separately identifiable psychiatric disorder and its impact on the perception of pain;

(viii) the age of the claimant;

(ix) prognosis.

(a) Complex Regional Pain Syndrome (CRPS)

The condition is characterized by intense, burning pain which can make moving or even touching the affected limb intolerable.

		with 10% uplift

(i) Severe: in such cases the prognosis will be poor; ability to work will be greatly reduced if not completely eliminated; significant care/domestic assistance needs; co-existing psychological problems may be present. At the top end of the scale, symptoms may have spread to other limbs.   £44,790 to £71,670   £49,270 to £78,840

75

		with 10% uplift

(ii) Moderate: the top end of this bracket will include cases where significant effects have been experienced for a prolonged period but prognosis assumes some future improvement enabling a return to work in a significant (not necessarily full-time) capacity and with only modest future care requirements. At the lower end will be cases where symptoms have persisted for some years but are more variable in intensity, where medication is effective in limiting symptoms, and/or where the prognosis is markedly better, though not necessarily for complete resolution. May already have resumed employment. Minimal, if any, future care requirements.

£23,910 to £44,790   £26,300 to £49,270

(b) **Other Pain Disorders**

£35,930 to £53,740   £39,530 to £59,110

(i) Severe: In these cases significant symptoms will be ongoing despite treatment and will be expected to persist, resulting in adverse impact on ability to work and the need for some care/assistance. Most cases of Fibromyalgia with serious persisting symptoms will fall within this range.

		with 10% uplift
(ii) Moderate: At the top end of this bracket are cases where symptoms are ongoing, albeit of lesser degree than in (i) above and the impact on ability to work/function in daily life is less marked. At the bottom end are cases where full, or near complete recovery has been made (or is anticipated) after symptoms have persisted for a number of years. Cases involving significant symptoms but where the claimant was vulnerable to the development of a pain disorder within a few years (or 'acceleration' cases) will also fall within this bracket.	£17,970 to £32,840	**£19,770 to £36,120**

9
Facial Injuries

The assessment of general damages for facial injuries is an extremely difficult task, there being three elements which complicate the award.

First, while in most of the cases dealt with below the injuries described are skeletal, many of them will involve an element of disfigurement or at least some cosmetic effect.

Second, in cases where there is a cosmetic element the courts have hitherto drawn a distinction between the awards of damages to males and females, the latter attracting significantly higher awards. That distinction, arising from cases that stretch back into the mists of time, has been reflected in succeeding editions of these Guidelines. Such distinction appears difficult to justify and has not been retained. In consequence the previous brackets have been merged and are currently wide and overlapping. They will be narrowed in future editions to the extent that judicial decisions warrant it.

Third, in cases of disfigurement there may also be severe psychological reactions which put the total award at the top of the bracket, or above it altogether.

(A) Skeletal Injuries

			with 10% uplift
(a)	Le Fort Fractures of Frontal Facial Bones	£20,320 to £31,350	£22,350 to £34,480
(b)	Multiple Fractures of Facial Bones Involving some facial deformity of a permanent nature.	£12,700 to £20,430	£13,970 to £22,470

with 10% uplift

(c)   Fractures of Nose or Nasal
       Complex

(i)	Serious or multiple fractures requiring a number of operations and/or resulting in permanent damage to airways, difficulty breathing, and/or nerves or tear ducts and/or facial deformity.	£9,080 to £19,730	£9,990 to £21,700
(ii)	Displaced fracture where recovery complete but only after surgery.	£3,370 to £4,350	£3,710 to £4,790
(iii)	Displaced fracture requiring no more than manipulation.	£2,160 to £2,690	£2,370 to £2,960
(iv)	Simple undisplaced fracture with full recovery.	£1,460 to £2,160	£1,600 to £2,370

(d)   Fractures of Cheekbones

(i)	Serious fractures requiring surgery but with lasting consequences such as paraesthesia in the cheeks or the lips or some element of disfigurement.	£8,700 to £13,470	£9,570 to £14,810
(ii)	Simple fracture of cheekbones for which some reconstructive surgery is necessary but from which there is a complete recovery with no or only minimal cosmetic effects.	£3,710 to £5,510	£4,080 to £6,060
(iii)	Simple fracture of cheekbone for which no surgery is required and where a complete recovery is effected.	£1,990 to £2,560	£2,180 to £2,810

(e) Fractures of Jaws

		with 10% uplift
(i) Very serious multiple fractures followed by prolonged treatment and permanent consequences, including severe pain, restriction in eating, paraesthesia, and/or the risk of arthritis in the joints.	£26,010 to £38,850	£28,610 to £42,730
(ii) Serious fracture with permanent consequences such as difficulty in opening the mouth or with eating or where there is paraesthesia in the area of the jaw.	£15,320 to £26,010	£16,860 to £28,610
(iii) Simple fracture requiring immobilization but from which recovery is complete.	£5,510 to £7,460	£6,060 to £8,200

(f) Damage to Teeth

In these cases there will generally have been a course of treatment as a result of the initial injury. The amounts awarded will vary according to the extent and/or the degree of discomfort of such treatment. Any difficulty with eating increases the award. These cases may overlap with fractures of the jaw, meriting awards in the brackets for such fractures. Awards may be greater where the damage results in or is caused by protracted dentistry.

Significant, chronic, tooth pain (such as from an untreated abscess) extending over a number of years together with significant general deterioration in the overall condition of teeth:	Up to £32,540	Up to £35,790
(i) Loss of or serious damage to several front teeth.	£7,460 to £9,740	£8,200 to £10,710

		with 10% uplift
(ii) Loss of or serious damage to two front teeth.	£3,710 to £6,510	£4,080 to £7,160
(iii) Loss of or serious damage to one front tooth.	£1,880 to £3,370	£2,070 to £3,710
(iv) Loss of or damage to back teeth: per tooth:	£930 to £1,460	£1,020 to £1,600

(B) Facial Disfigurement

In this class of case a number of common factors fall to be considered:

- the nature of the underlying injury which has resulted in facial disfigurement;
- the nature and extent of treatment;
- the nature and extent of the residual scarring or disfigurement;
- the age of the claimant;
- the subjective impact of the disfigurement upon the claimant including the extent to which they valued their appearance;
- the extent to which the injury adversely affects the claimant's social, domestic, and work lives;
- the psychological impact upon the claimant, which in severe cases may be very substantial.

The subject of burns is not dealt with separately. Burns of any degree of severity are particularly painful and disfiguring, and awards are invariably at the upper ends of the brackets, or above them altogether. The very worst burns may lead not only to considerable disfigurement and pain but to a variety of continuing physical and psychological injuries meriting very high awards. See also the general guidance in relation to burn injuries in Chapter 10.

As explained earlier, it is doubtful that gender alone can justify different levels of award.

			with 10% uplift
(a)	**Very Severe Scarring**	£25,400 to £83,050	**£27,940 to £91,350**

In relatively young claimants (typically teens to early 30s), where the cosmetic effect is very disfiguring and the psychological reaction severe.

(b)	**Less Severe Scarring**	£15,320 to £41,310	**£16,860 to £45,440**

Where the disfigurement is still substantial and where there is a significant psychological reaction.

(c)	**Significant Scarring**	£7,780 to £25,670	**£8,550 to £28,240**

Where the worst effects have been or will be reduced by plastic surgery leaving some cosmetic disability and where the psychological reaction is not great or, having been considerable at the outset, has diminished to relatively minor proportions. Will include cases where the scarring is visible at conversational distance.

		with 10% uplift

(d) Less Significant Scarring

In these cases there may be but one scar which can be camouflaged or, though there is a number of very small scars, the overall effect is to mar but not markedly to affect the appearance and the reaction is no more than that of an ordinarily sensitive young person.

£3,370 to £11,730 — £3,710 to £12,900

(e) Trivial Scarring

In these cases the effect is minor only.

£1,460 to £3,010 — £1,600 to £3,310

10

Scarring to Other Parts of the Body

This is an area in which it is not possible to offer much useful guidance. The principles (including the approach to awards for different genders) are the same as those applied to cases of facial disfigurement. It must be remembered that many of the physical injuries already described involve some element of disfigurement and that element is of course taken into account in suggesting the appropriate bracket. There remain some cases where the element of disfigurement is the predominant one in the assessment of damages. Where the scarring is not to the face or is not usually visible then the awards will tend to be lower than those for facial or readily visible disfigurement.

		with 10% uplift
A large proportion of awards for a number of noticeable laceration scars, or a single disfiguring scar, of leg(s) or arm(s) or hand(s) or back or chest fall in the bracket of £6,680 to £19,390 (**£7,350** to **£21,330** with uplift).	£6,680 to £19,390	**£7,350 to £21,330**
In cases where an exploratory laparotomy has been performed but no significant internal injury has been found, the award reflects the operation and the inevitable scar.	In the region of £7,380	**In the region of £8,110**
A single noticeable scar, or several superficial scars, of leg(s) or arm(s) or hand(s), with some minor cosmetic deficit.	£2,020 to £6,680	**£2,220 to £7,350**

As we have noted in Chapter 9, the effects of burns will normally be regarded as more serious since they tend to cause a greater degree of pain and may lead to continuing physical and psychological injury. Serious burn injuries will attract very significant awards. Where significant burns cover 40% or more of the body, awards are likely to exceed £89,440 (**£98,380** accounting for 10% uplift). Factors which will influence the size of award in burns cases will include:

	with 10% uplift
Likely to exceed £89,440	Likely to exceed £98,380

(a) The percentage body area affected by the burns;

(b) Whether the burns are full thickness, partial thickness, or superficial;

(c) The cosmetic impact of the injuries and the injured person's reactions to them;

(d) The need for (and extent of) surgery;

(e) Any resulting physical disability;

(f) The psychological impact.

11

Damage to Hair

	with 10% uplift

(a) Damage to hair in consequence of defective permanent waving, tinting, or the like, where the effects are dermatitis, eczema, or tingling or 'burning' of the scalp causing dry, brittle hair, which breaks off and/or falls out, leading to distress, depression, embarrassment, and loss of confidence, and inhibiting social life. In the more serious cases thinning continues and the prospects of regrowth are poor or there has been total loss of areas of hair and regrowth is slow.

£6,260 to £9,400   **£6,890 to £10,340**

There may be a larger award in cases of significant psychological disability or if surgical intervention (e.g. skin grafting) is required.

(b) Less serious versions of the above where symptoms are fewer or only of a minor character; also, cases where hair has been pulled out leaving bald patches. The level of the award will depend on the length of time taken before regrowth occurs. This bracket will include cases of alopecia induced by stress causing some hair loss where full recovery is made within two years.

£3,370 to £6,260   **£3,710 to £6,890**

12

Dermatitis and Other Skin Conditions

Apart from dermatitis of the scalp (see Chapter 11), most of the reported cases relate to dermatitis of the hands. Higher awards are likely to be justified where the face is affected. This chapter also includes other skin conditions such as eczema and psoriasis.

			with 10% uplift
(a)	Dermatitis of both hands, with cracking and soreness, affecting employment and domestic capability, possibly with some psychological consequences, lasting for some years, perhaps indefinitely.	£11,730 to £16,380	**£12,900 to £18,020**
(b)	Dermatitis of one or both hands, continuing for a significant period, but settling with treatment and/or use of gloves for specific tasks.	£7,380 to £9,740	**£8,110 to £10,710**
(c)	Itching, irritation of, and/or rashes on one or both hands, but resolving within a few months with treatment. A short-lived aggravation of a pre-existing skin condition will also fall within this bracket.	£1,460 to £3,370	**£1,600 to £3,710**

13

Minor Injuries

Minor injuries are injuries which are of short duration, where there is a complete recovery within three months, and are not otherwise referred to in other chapters. Cases where there is significant pain or multiple injuries albeit full recovery within three months may fall outside this chapter. Likewise cases involving, for example, travel anxiety (associated with minor physical injuries) or minor scarring where symptoms last for more than three months may appropriately be included in this chapter. The awards within each bracket will be dependent on the severity and duration of symptoms. The extent to which the level of symptoms remains relatively constant will also be a relevant factor. Claims solely in respect of shock or travel anxiety in the absence of physical or recognized psychiatric injury will not attract an award of compensation.

In respect of whiplash injuries falling within this category please refer to the note in the introduction to these guidelines and to the introduction at Chapter 7.

			with 10% uplift
(a)	Injuries where there is a complete recovery within seven days.	A few hundred pounds to £590	A few hundred pounds to £650
(b)	Injuries where there is a complete recovery within 28 days.	£590 to £1,170	£650 to £1,290
(c)	Injuries where there is a complete recovery within three months.	£1,170 to £2,090	£1,290 to £2,300

Index